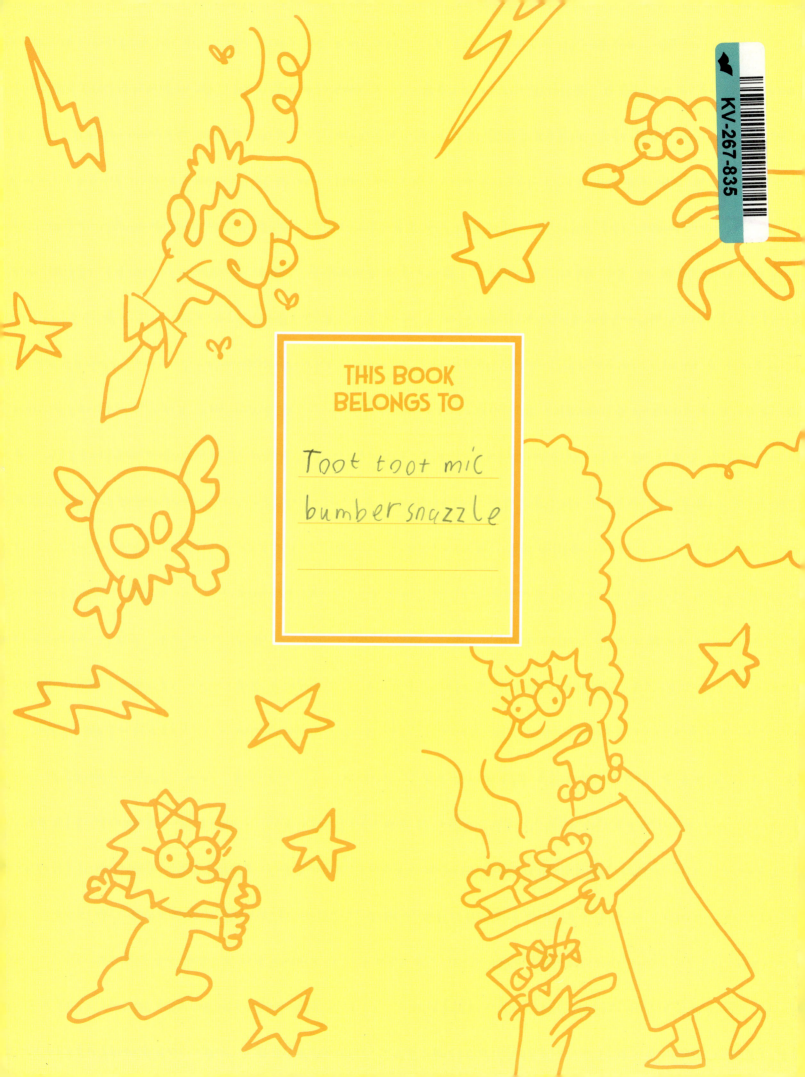

THIS BOOK
BELONGS TO

Toot toot mic
bumbersnazzle

BART SIMPSON 2015 ANNUAL

Copyright © 2014
Bongo Entertainment, Inc. All rights reserved.
No part of this book may be used or reproduced in any manner whatsoever
without written permission except in the case of brief quotations
embodied in critical articles and reviews. For information address
Bongo Comics Group
P.O. Box 1963, Santa Monica, CA 90406-1963

Published in the UK by Titan Books, a division of Titan Publishing Group,
144 Southwark St., London SE1 0UP, under licence from Bongo Entertainment, Inc.

FIRST EDITION: SEPTEMBER 2014

ISBN 9781783294497

2 4 6 8 10 9 7 5 3 1

Publisher: Matt Groening
Creative Director: Nathan Kane
Managing Editor: Terry Delegeane
Director of Operations: Robert Zaugh
Art Director: Chia-Hsien Jason Ho
Art Director Special Projects: Serban Cristescu
Production Manager: Christopher Ungar
Assistant Art Director: Mike Rote
Assistant Editor: Karen Bates
Colors: Nathan Hamill, Art Villanueva
Administration: Ruth Waytz, Pete Benson
Legal Guardian: Susan A. Grode

PRINTED IN ITALY

BART SIMPSON
2015 ANNUAL

MATT GROENING

TITAN BOOKS

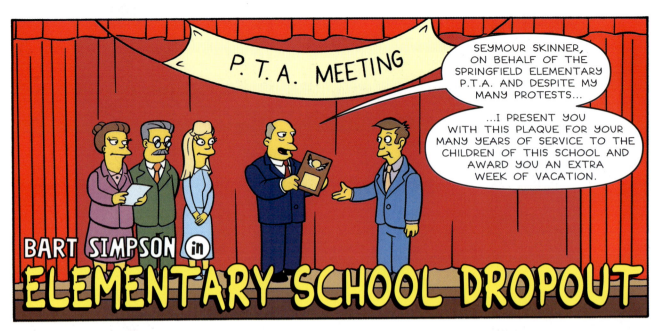

EARL KRESS
SCRIPT

JOEY NILGES
PENCILS

ANDREW PEPOY
INKS

NATHAN HAMILL
COLORS

KAREN BATES
LETTERS

BILL MORRISON
EDITOR

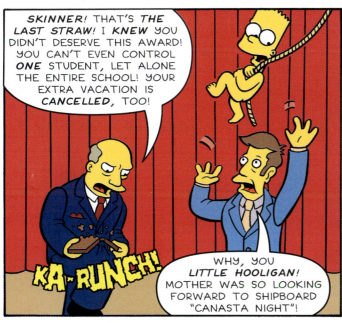

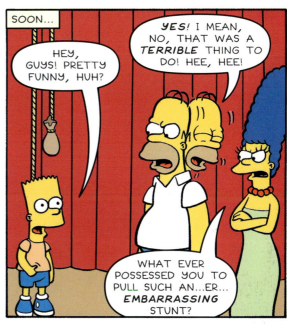

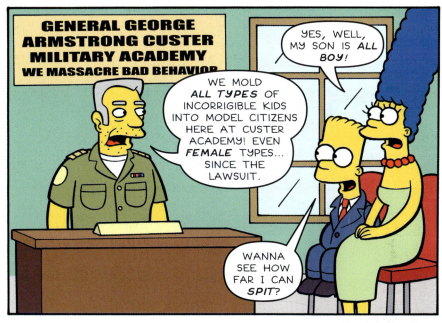

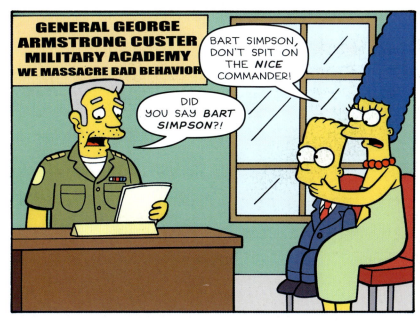

9

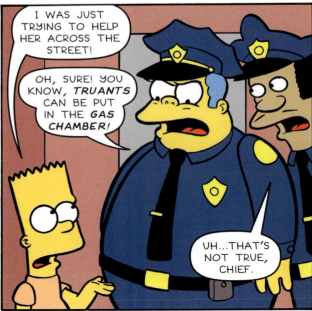

SIMPSON! WHAT ARE *YOU* DOING IN THE SANCTITY OF *MY* HOME? IS HE *HURTING* YOU, MOTHER?

KEEP YOUR SHRUNKEN PANTS ON, SEYMOUR! BART WAS *HELPING* ME WITH THE GROCERIES.

OKAY, YOU HELPED! NOW GO BACK TO THE LEVEL OF HELL YOU CAME FROM, DEMON CHILD!

SEYMOUR! DON'T SPEAK TO OUR *GUEST* THAT WAY! HE'S JOINING US FOR *DINNER* AND AFTER THAT...PARCHEESI!!

I NEVER TRIED PARCHEESI BEFORE. CAN I HAVE *WHIPPED CREAM* ON MINE?

BART WON'T BE HOME TONIGHT.

WOO-HOO! MORE FOOD FOR *ME!*

DON'T YOU THINK IT'S *ODD* THAT BART IS STAYING AT PRINCIPAL SKINNER'S HOUSE?

NOPE. MORE FOOD FOR ME! WOO-HOO!

HEY, SEYMOUR, YOUR FLY'S OPEN!

NO, IT'S NOT.

MADE YOU LOOK!

IT WAS *BAD ENOUGH* AT SCHOOL, NOW HE'S *DISRESPECTING* ME IN MY OWN HOUSE!

IT'S *MY* HOUSE...AND *LIGHTEN UP,* SEYMOUR! IT WAS JUST A LITTLE JOKE!

VERY LITTLE JOKE! DINNER'S OVER, TIME TO *GO HOME!*

IT'S *TOO LATE* FOR HIM TO GO HOME! I THINK HE SHOULD *STAY HERE* TONIGHT!

GO UPSTAIRS AND RUN MY BATH WATER, BART!

THAT'S SUPPOSED TO BE *MY JOB,* MOTHER!

GET OVER IT, SEYMOUR! AND ZIP UP YOUR FLY!

MY FLY'S NOT...

MADE YOU LOOK! HAR, HAR! ⸨COUGH! COUGH!⸩

WHAT ARE YOU DOING WEARING *MY* PAJAMAS!

GETTING READY TO SLEEP IN *YOUR* BED. WHAT DOES IT LOOK LIKE?

THE NEXT DAY...

I WENT TO GET YOUR CLEANING, MOTHER, BUT THEY SAID IT HAD *ALREADY* BEEN PICKED UP.

WHAT IS *HE* DOING HERE *AGAIN*?

HE PICKED UP THE CLEANING! YOU GOT A PROBLEM?

AND THE NEXT DAY...

AGAIN?!?

YO, SEYMOUR! YOU'RE OUT OF *FRUIT JUICE!*

GLUG!

WHY ARE YOU OVER HERE *ALL THE TIME*?

I DUNNO. MAYBE IF I HAD *SOMEPLACE ELSE* TO BE!

BART, IF I LET YOU RETURN TO SCHOOL, WILL YOU *STOP* COMING AROUND HERE?

OKAY BY ME.

THANKS, MRS. S! THAT WAS AN *AWE-SOME PLAN* YOU HAD TO GET ME BACK IN SCHOOL!

SEYMOUR! YOU CERTAINLY HANDLED THAT LITTLE SCALAWAG!

AND IT WAS *FUN* ANNOYING SEYMOUR, TOO...*DUDE!*

THE END

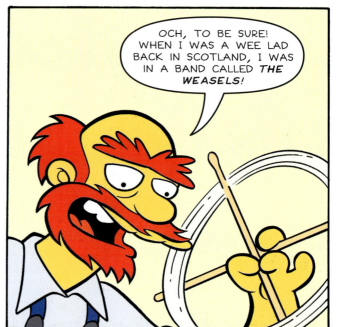

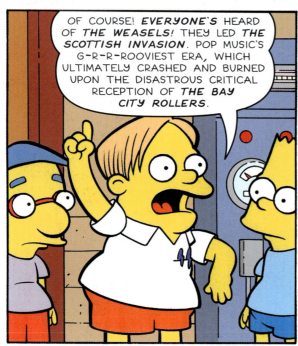

"IT WAS THE HEY DAY OF WEASELMANIA!"

"WE HAD DUNCAN MCGREGOR ON THE BASS GUITAR..."

I'M THE WILY, WHEEDLING WEASEL!

"ANGUS MCDUFF ON LEAD GUITAR..."

I'M THE WEAK, WIMPY WEASEL!

"GEORDIE MCINTYRE ON THE BAGPIPES..."

I'M THE WEIRD, WHEEZY WEASEL!

"AND ME, WEE WILLIE, ON THE DRUMS."

I'M THE WISE, WITTY WEASEL!

"WE RELEASED OUR FIRST RECORD, **ME LOVE'S IN THE LOO,** AND IT WENT STRAIGHT TO NUMBER ONE IN SCOTLAND!"

"WE COULD NAE WALK THE STREETS OF GLASGOW, EDINBURGH, OR ABERDEEN WITHOUT BEING MOBBED."

"I WAS NOT THEN THE COARSE GALOOT YOU SEE BEFORE YOU. BACK THEN, I HAD A MOST AGREEABLE COUNTENANCE, AND, I DARE SAY, I WAS A BIT OF A DANDY."

"I WAS THE FIRST TO WEAR A MINI-KILT."

"AND IT WAS *I* WHO INVENTED *THE WEASEL HAIRCUT*...BRUSHING ME EYEBROWS UP AND OVER ME FOREHEAD."

"*OCH!* BUT MY FASHION SENSE AND CHARISMA WAS MY UNDOING. YOU SEE, ALL THE LASSIES WERE MAD FOR ME."

"I AVERAGED OVER 800 MARRIAGE PROPOSALS A DAY!"

Dear Willie,
Marry me and
...y for free!

Fiona McFadden
Stewardess,
Air Scotland

"I'D SHAKE MY HEAD AND GO "WOOOOOO," AND THE BONNIE GIRLS WOULD SCREAM AND THROW HAGGIS UP ON THE STAGE."

WILLIE! WON'T HE?

WEE LOVE WEE WILLIE!

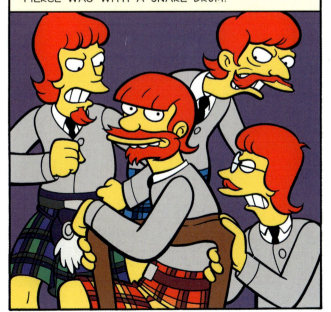

THE OTHER WEASELS COULDN'T STAND IT. JEALOUS THEY WERE OF ME GOOD LOOKS AND FIERCE WAY WITH A SNARE DRUM."

"AND SO, WHILST ON OUR FIRST TRIP TO AMERI-CA, THEY DITCHED ME HERE IN SPRINGFIELD AND REPLACED ME WITH SOME LIVERPUDLIAN IDIOT. "BLINGO" THEY CALLED HIM, BECAUSE OF ALL THE JEWELRY HE WORE."

AND THAT'S HOW I CAME TO LIVE IN YOUR FAIR CITY.

AN EPIC TALE OF FAME, FORTUNE, AND BETRAYAL!

WOW! YOU WERE KICKED OUT OF THE GREATEST, MOST POPULAR BAND OF ALL TIME!

THOSE WEASELS WERE REAL WEASELS, WILLIE! NO WONDER YOU'RE SO *BITTER.*

BITTER? NOT ME! NAE. I'LL TELL YOU WHO'S BITTER...MY FORMER BAND MATE, SIR DUNCAN MCGREGOR, THE RICHEST MAN IN SCOTLAND."

"I'VE HAD A RICH AND VARIED LIFE WHILE SIR DUNCAN'S BEEN STUCK SINGING *ME LOVE'S IN THE LOO* FOR THE LAST THIRTY-SOMETHIN' YEARS."

♪ BOO, HOO! ♪ WHAT'S A LAD TO DO? ME LOVE'S IN ♪ THE LOO. ♪

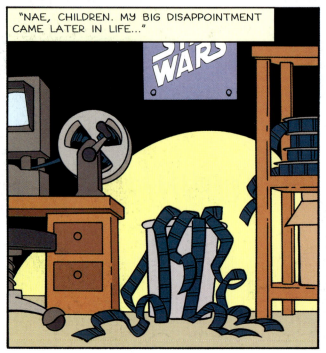

"NAE, CHILDREN. MY BIG DISAPPOINTMENT CAME LATER IN LIFE..."

"...WHEN MY MOTION PICTURE DEBUT ENDED UP ON THE CUTTING ROOM FLOOR."

THE END

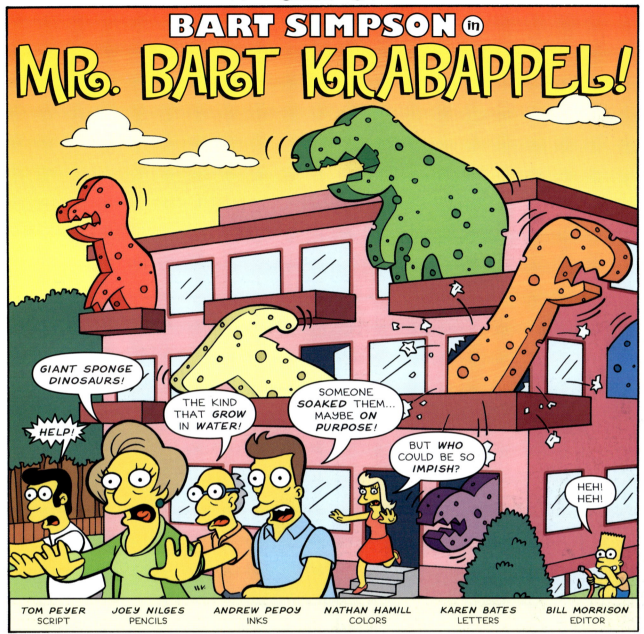

ALL RIGHT...MRS. KRABAPPEL KEPT ME AFTER SCHOOL, *OK*? FOR *NO GOOD REASON*!

HERE YOU GO, MISTER! NOW SCRUB THAT *GUM* OUT!

EXCUSE ME, TEACHER...

¡GROOOAN!¡

...HAVE YOU TAUGHT YOUR KIDS ABOUT *SPONGE DINOSAURS* THAT GROW IN *WATER*? JUST $12.99 A GROSS, AND THEY'RE *LOADED* WITH SCIENCE!

NO SOLICITORS! GET LOST!

AWWW, BUT GIL *NEEDS* THIS SALE!

TOUGH! I ALREADY HAVE *CASES* OF THOSE *JUNKOSAURS* CLUTTERING MY BASEMENT!

OH?

BOY'S STORY CHECKS OUT. KRABAPPEL IMPROPERLY STORED *TONS* OF FREE EDUCATIONAL SAMPLES. THOSE ABSORBENT *THUNDER LIZARDS* WERE A *RAMPAGE* WAITING TO *HAPPEN*.

TEACHERS. WHEN WILL THEY *LEARN*?

DON'T BLAME *KRABAPPEL*, CHIEF! BLAME THE *BOY*!

WE TOWNS-PEOPLE TEND TO *AGREE*!

AYE! WE ARE *USED* TO BLAMING YOUNG BART, AND FAMILIAR THINGS *SOOTHE* US!

FAIR ENOUGH! BART SIMPSON, I HEREBY *CONVICT* YOU OF INCITING A *MONSTER STAMPEDE!* SINCE YOU'VE WATERLOGGED YOUR TEACHER'S HOME...

...I SENTENCE YOU TO *LET* HER MOVE IN WITH YOU!

AAAAHH!

D'OH!

THE NEXT DAY...

DAD, HOW CAN YOU LET THIS *HAPPEN* TO ME? I NEED MY AFTER SCHOOL TIME TO *UNWIND!* NOW I'LL *NEVER* GET ANY PEACE!

DON'T BE A *BABY!* IT ISN'T *THAT* BAD! I REMEMBER WHEN I WAS YOUR--

THERE SHE IS! SIT UP STRAIGHT AND HIDE THE SQUISHEE!

SKREEECH

SOON...

NO *RUNNING* IN THE *HOUSE*, MISTER!

IS THIS THE KIND OF *TRASH* YOU WATCH ON TV?

YOU SHOULD BE IN *BED* BY NOW!

YOU'RE NOT EVEN *LISTENING!* WHAT DID I JUST *SAY?*

THAT'S NOT HOW YOU DO IT! GIVE ME YOUR TOOTH-BRUSH, AND *I'LL* SHOW YOU!

NO, YOU'RE *NOT* GOING OUT!

YOU WILL *SIT* UNTIL YOU KNOW THOSE MULTIPLICATION TABLES BY *HEART!*

27

LISA, HAVE YOU SEEN YOUR *FATHER*? I NEED HIM TO CLAP THESE *ERASERS*.

UHHH...

YAAAH...!

OW!

AGGH!

AHRR!

OWWW!

AAGHHH!

SORRY WE HAD TO MEET THIS WAY, DAD, BUT I COULDN'T LET KRABAPPEL SEE US.

I THINK I KNOW HOW TO GET *RID* OF HER. I'LL NEED YOUR *HELP*, AND SOME WORKING CAPITAL. SAY...$12.99?

I'M LISTENING.

THE END

WITH GREAT POWER...

MAN, HOW COOL WOULD IT BE TO HAVE *SUPER POWERS*?

YOU GET TO FLY AROUND, PUNCH STUFF, AND BE ALL HEROIC!

AND YOU DON'T HAVE TO LIVE IN CONSTANT, PARALYZING *FEAR* OF CONSTANT, PARALYZING *WEDGIES!*

MAX DAVISON WRITER   **NINA MATSUMOTO** PENCILS   **ANDREW PEPOY** INKS   **NATHAN HAMILL** COLORS   **KAREN BATES** LETTERS   **NATHAN KANE** EDITOR

BUT SUPERHEROES ONLY GET POWERS FROM *FREAK ACCIDENTS*.

LOOK AT *RADIOACTIVE MAN!* HE WAS CLAUDE KANE III, JUST A HIGH-SOCIETY, LAYABOUT PLAYBOY!

#1 RADIOACTIVE MAN

THE RETOLD UNTOLD ORIGIN!

MATT GROENING

"BUT THEN HE GOT CAUGHT IN A *NUCLEAR EXPLOSION* AND BECAME THE GREATEST HERO EVER!"

KABOOM!

¡CHOKE!; I HAVE BECOME A... *RADIOACTIVE MAN!*

HMMM. YOU'RE RIGHT. SUPERHEROES NEVER *WANT* TO GET POWERS. BUT *WE DO!*

WHAT ARE YOU THINKING?

LET'S GIVE *OURSELVES* SUPER POWERS!

WE'VE SEEN HOW IT HAPPENS IN THE COMICS, SO WE JUST HAVE TO FOLLOW THEIR LEAD!

YOU MEAN, LIKE JOINING THE ARMY AND HOPING THEY PUT US IN THE *SUPER SOLDIER* PROGRAM?

NAH. I HEARD ALL SUPER SCIENCE GOT SLASHED IN THE LAST ROUND OF GOVERNMENT CUTS.
BUT I DEFINITELY KNOW WHERE WE CAN FIND SOME *SCIENCE GONE WRONG!*

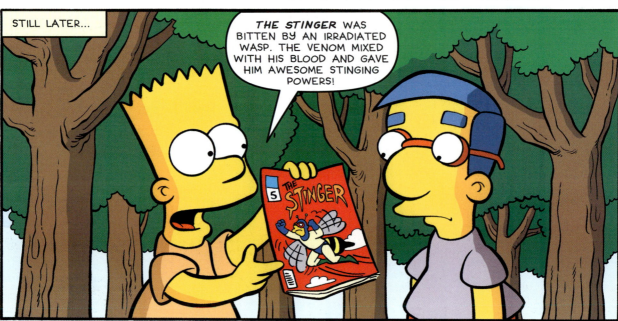

34

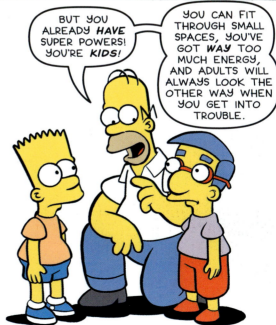

BART SIMPSON IN
ONE FOR ALL AND ALPHA ONE

HEY, BART, LET'S PRETEND LIKE WE'RE ARCHEOLOGISTS AND THIS IS OUR DIG.

I CAN DIG IT, MAN!

MATT GROENING

FUTURE HOME OF SPRINGFIELD'S
GARAGE MAHAL LUXURY ESTATES!
"A COMMITMENT TO EXCELLENCE FAR BEYOND YOUR OWN BOORISH PERSONAL TASTES."

WHOA! WHAT'S *THIS*?!

IT LOOKS LIKE SOME KIND OF OLD BOOK.

DIRT IS FULL OF MINERALS!

MARY TRAINOR	JAMES LLOYD	ANDREW PEPOY	NATHAN HAMILL	KAREN BATES	BILL MORRISON
SCRIPT	PENCILS	INKS	COLORS	LETTERS	EDITOR

SO WHO WERE THESE GUYS AND HOW DID THEY GET LOST?

LONG, LONG AGO THERE WAS A TRIBE OF GENTLE PEOPLE LIVING PEACEFULLY IN THE FIELD OF SPRINGS...

"LEGEND HAS IT THAT THESE MEEK AND MELLOW FOLK WERE DRIVEN FROM THEIR LAND BY A FIERCE BAND OF RAPACIOUS DEVELOPERS."

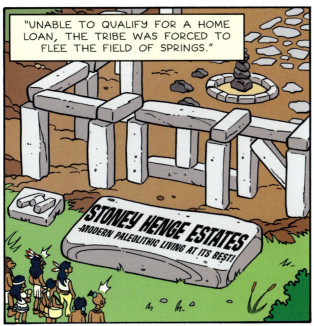

"UNABLE TO QUALIFY FOR A HOME LOAN, THE TRIBE WAS FORCED TO FLEE THE FIELD OF SPRINGS."

STONEY HENGE ESTATES
-MODERN PALEOLITHIC LIVING AT ITS BEST!

"THEY DISPERSED THROUGHOUT THE LAND, HOLDING FIRM IN THE BELIEF THAT THEY WOULD RETURN SOMEDAY. IT WAS SAID THAT THE TRIBE WOULD BE LOST FOR A THOUSAND YEARS...UNTIL THEIR PROPHET RETURNED TO RETRIEVE THEIR TRIBAL BIBLE."

THIS TRIBAL BIBLE!

"...AND VERILY YOUR TRIBE SHALL REMAINETH LOST UNTIL THE CHOSEN ONE DOTH COMETH FORTH HE IS YOUR ALPHA MEN." WHOA!!! MILHOUSE AND I MUST BE THE ALPHA MEN!

POSSIBLY. BUT, THE TRIBAL BIBLE FORETELLS OF A CHOSEN ONE, NOT TWO. AMONG BABOONS, AND I USE THE TERM ADVISEDLY, THIS WOULD REFER TO THE ALPHA MALE.

OBVIOUSLY WE NEED A *THIRD* ALPHA MAN TO BREAK THIS STALEMATE.

I VOTE WE BEGIN CANVASSING IMMEDIATELY FOR A NEW MEMBER.

AND SO...

SORRY. I'VE GOT JAZZERCISE CLASS.

NO, SORRY. I'VE GOT A STRUDEL IN DER OVEN.

GET LOST, DWEEBS. I'M BUSY LOITERING WITH INTENT.

SORRY, DUDES, I'VE GOT 846 HOURS OF COMMUNITY SERVICE TO PERFORM.

NO, THANK YOU. SECRET SOCIETIES ARE TOOLS OF SATAN.

SORRY. I'M BOOKED UP SOLID UNTIL 8TH GRADE.

OOOH, NO. MEMBERSHIP MAKES ME QUEASY.

AND SO BART AND MILHOUSE END UP WITH...

43

44

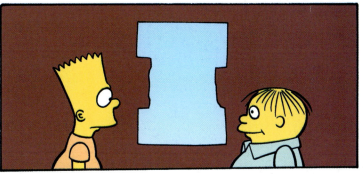

"HE IS YOUR ALPHA MEN." ODD. THAT'S SUCH POOR SYNTAX! THE ANCIENTS WERE KNOWN FOR THEIR GRAMMATICAL EXCELLENCE AND YET THESE WRITINGS ARE SORELY LACKING IN PUNCTUATION.

NOW, IF ONE WERE TO ADD A COMMA HERE AND A PERIOD THERE, THAT LAST SENTENCE WOULD READ...

"HE IS YOU, RALPH. AMEN."

HI, LISA! CAN I HAVE MY BOOK BACK NOW?

SURE. HERE YOU GO!

TOSS!

I'M IN THE LOCUST POSITION!

THE END

BART SIMPSON IN PRINCIPAL SIMPSON!

TOM PEYER	MIKE DECARLO	KEN WHEATON	ROBERT STANLEY	KAREN BATES	BILL MORRISON
SCRIPT	PENCILS	INKS	COLORS	LETTERS	EDITOR

LATER...

CLASS, I'D LIKE TO INTRODUCE A NEW STUDENT...*SEYMOUR SKINNER.* TRY TO *FORGET* THAT HE ONCE HAD THE POWER TO *PUNISH* YOU...

EDNA, *PLEASE.*

...AND THAT HE AND I WERE ONCE ENGAGED TO BE *MARRIED* UNTIL HE BITTERLY *DISAPPOINTED* ME.

JUST TREAT HIM AS YOU WOULD ANY *OTHER* NEW CLASSMATE.

EDNA!

OH, NO...

NOW, I HAVE TO LEAVE THE ROOM...

NO!

...FOR AN *HOUR* OR SO.

FOR THE LOVE OF GOD, EDNA!

EDNAAAA...!

DEAL ME *IN,* BOYS! I'M FEELIN' *LUCKY* TODAY!

TEACHER'S LOUNGE

PROBLEM, SEYMOUR?

IT WAS SO *AWFUL*! THEY HAD *TAPE*!

FRANKLY, I DON'T KNOW *HOW* TO MAKE YOU GET ALONG WITH OTHERS. MAYBE WE NEED...

...A PARENT CONFERENCE.

NOOO!

SOON...

SO WE'RE *AGREED*, MRS. SKINNER?

YES! MY SEYMOUR IS A TERRIBLE, AWFUL BOY!

OWWWW!

NO...ABOUT THE *OTHER* THING.

OH, YEAH. IF HE'S GOING TO BE SUCH A BIG *CRY-BABY*...

MOTHER, I'M NOT A--

...YOU CAN GO AHEAD AND KICK HIS DIAPERED *HEINIE* BACK TO *KINDERGARTEN*!

54

¡GROOOAN!¡

TO *HECK* WITH *THIS.*

...AND THEN THEY *WRAPPED* ME WITH *DUCT TAPE!*

YOU KNOW WHAT *YOUR* PROBLEM IS, SEYMOUR? YOU *CARE* TOO MUCH! YOU DON'T SEE *BART* WORRY-ING ABOUT PEOPLE WRAPPING *HIM!*

BUT I COULD NEVER BE AS FANCY-FREE AS BART...!

BLAST IT, MAN! YOU ALREADY *ARE!* REMEMBER HOW *GOOD* YOU FELT WHEN YOU CAME TO LUNCH? IT WASN'T THE *CHALK DUST,* IT WAS THE *PUNISHMENT!* YOU *DUG* BEING THE *BAD BOY!*

BLAM!

I... *DID!* YOU'RE *RIGHT!*

MILHOUSE, THERE ARE *TWO HOURS* LEFT IN MY SCHOOL-BOY CAREER! *TWO HOURS* TO PLAN AND EXECUTE THE BIGGEST, LOUDEST, MESSIEST *PRANK* THIS INSTITUTION HAS EVER--

ATTENTION! ATTENTION!

THE END

56

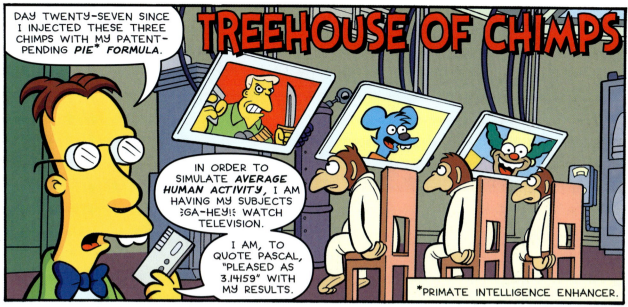

TREEHOUSE OF CHIMPS

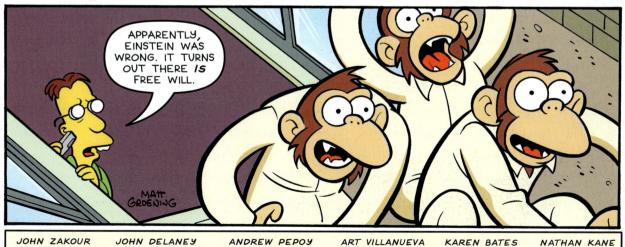

JOHN ZAKOUR
WRITER

JOHN DELANEY
PENCILS

ANDREW PEPOY
INKS

ART VILLANUEVA
COLORS

KAREN BATES
LETTERS

NATHAN KANE
EDITOR

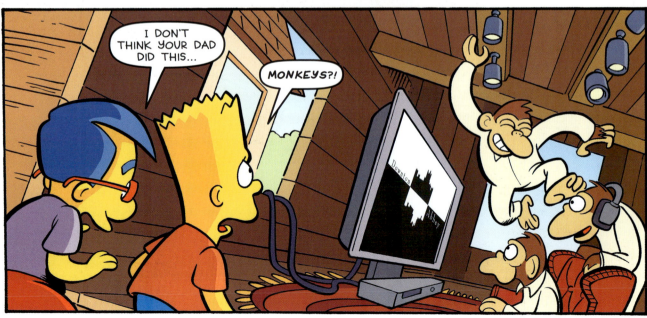

58

59

SO YOU'RE HAVING A PROBLEM WITH PRIMATES, EH? I READ ON PROFESSOR FRINK'S BLOG THAT HE'S BEEN EXPERIMENTING WITH CHIMPANZEES.

I'LL JUST TEXT HIM AND SEE.

SOON...

YES, THOSE ARE MY CHIMPS, BY GLAVIN. BUT I'M AFRAID I CAN'T HELP YOU.

WHY NOT?

MY EXPERIMENT WAS MERELY THE CATALYST. I MADE A BETTER CHIMP! IT'S UP TO THEM TO FIND A PLACE IN THE WORLD!

WELL, THEY CAN'T STAY IN MY TREEHOUSE!

THAT'S FOR *NATURAL SELECTION* TO DECIDE. GOOD LUCK, CHILDREN!

SEE, I *KNEW* SCIENCE WASN'T GOOD FOR ANY- THING!

I'LL BE IN MY ROOM.

OKAY, WE'VE GOT TO DO THE *ONE THING* HUMANS DO BETTER THAN EVERY OTHER ANIMAL... *SENSELESS VIOLENCE.*

I DON'T KNOW, BART. I SAW THIS MOVIE ONCE THAT SAID CHIMPS ARE A LOT *STRONGER* THAN THEY LOOK.

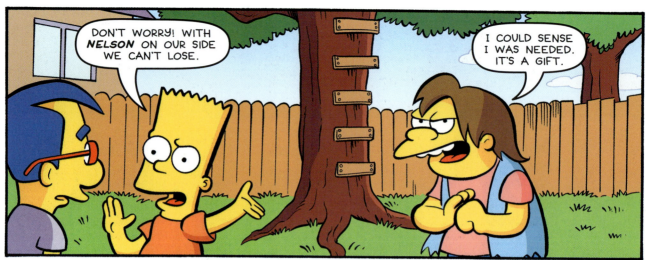

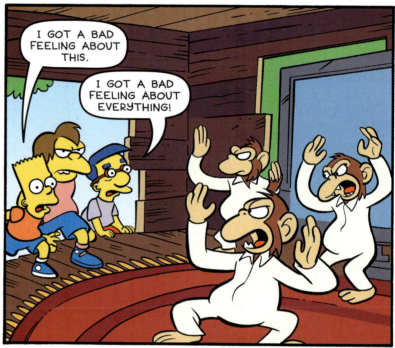

64

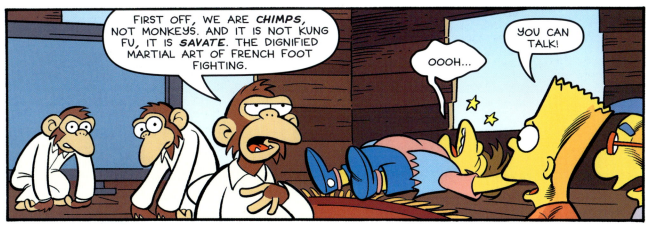

FIRST OFF, WE ARE **CHIMPS**, NOT MONKEYS. AND IT IS NOT KUNG FU, IT IS **SAVATE**. THE DIGNIFIED MARTIAL ART OF FRENCH FOOT FIGHTING.

OOOH...

YOU CAN TALK!

OF COURSE WE CAN! IF **YOU** CAN DO IT, HOW HARD CAN IT REALLY BE?

HE'S GOT US THERE.

GOSH, BART! THESE CHIMPS SEEM LIKE INTELLIGENT, REASONABLE CREATURES.

WELL, WE **DO** HAVE ONLINE DEGREES FROM THE **UNIVERSITY OF PHOENIX!**

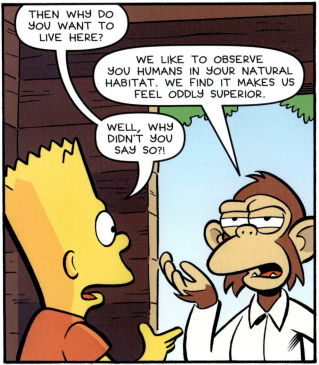

THEN WHY DO YOU WANT TO LIVE HERE?

WE LIKE TO OBSERVE YOU HUMANS IN YOUR NATURAL HABITAT. WE FIND IT MAKES US FEEL ODDLY SUPERIOR.

WELL, WHY DIDN'T YOU SAY SO?!

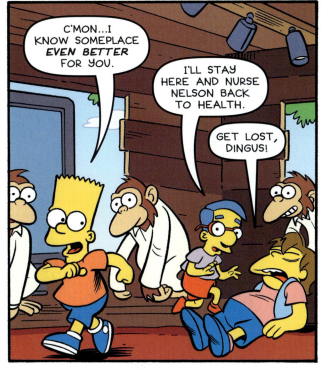

C'MON...I KNOW SOMEPLACE **EVEN BETTER** FOR YOU.

I'LL STAY HERE AND NURSE NELSON BACK TO HEALTH.

GET LOST, DINGUS!

66

SIMPSONS SHINDIG!

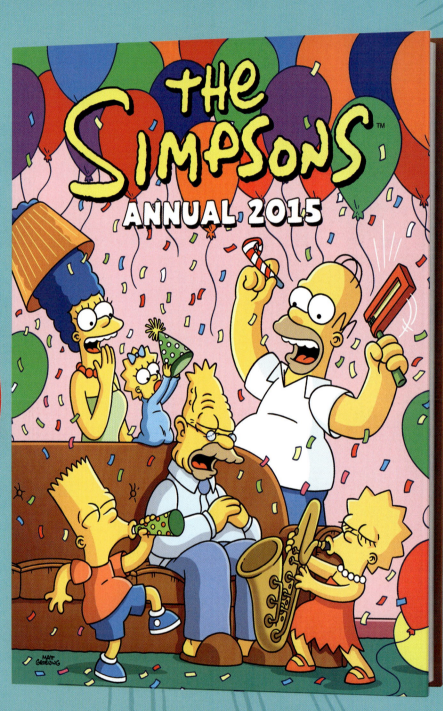

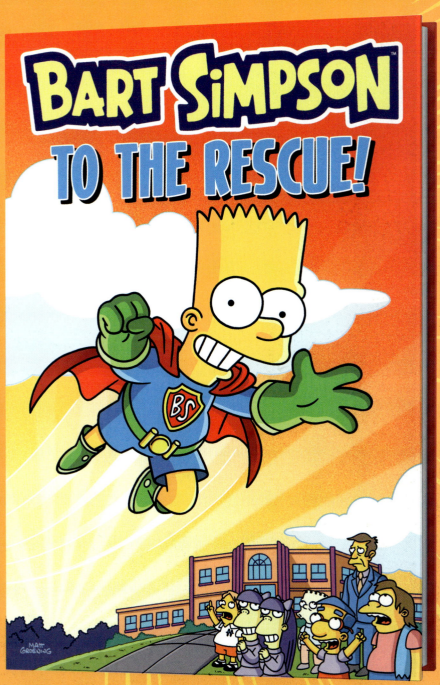